FACEHUNTER

FACEHUNTER

YVAN RODIC

with 326 color illustrations

PRESTEL

MUNICH | BERLIN | LONDON | NEW YORK

ON THE COVER **REYKJAVIK** Iceland Airwaves Festival October
BACK COVER **LONDON** Soho June
PREVIOUS SPREAD **REYKJAVIK** Downtown July

▶ **LONDON** Soho August

Thanks Mom and Dad.

Published by arrangement with Thames & Hudson Ltd, London
Copyright © 2010 Yvan Rodic
Photographs copyright © 2010 Yvan Rodic

First published simultaneously in 2010 in the United Kingdom
by Thames & Hudson Ltd, London and in the United States by Prestel Verlag,
a member of Verlagsgruppe Random House GmbH

Prestel Publishing
900 Broadway, Suite 603
New York, NY 10003
Tel. +1 (212) 995-2720
Fax +1 (212) 995-2733
www.prestel.com

Library of Congress Control Number is available.

Prestel books are available worldwide. Please contact your nearest bookseller
or one of the above addresses for information concerning your local distributor.

Printed and bound by C&C Offset Printing Co., Ltd, China

ISBN 978-3-7913-4453-9

"IS FACE HUNTING A SOCIOLOGICAL EXPERIMENT, OR JUST YOUR DAY JOB?"

GLOBALIZATION IS A MYTH. The belief that international brands and pop culture are making the world a standardized society populated by clones is an old-skool science-fiction vision of the future, not the reality of the 21st century.

Last year my itinerary took me to: Antwerp, Århus, Bandung, Barcelona, Berlin, Brussels, Bucharest, Copenhagen, Edinburgh, Emmaboda, Glasgow, Gothenburg, Helsinki, Istanbul, Jakarta, London, Malmö, Melbourne, Mexico City, Montreal, Moscow, Munich, New York, Paris, Reykjavík, São Paulo, Singapore, Stockholm, Sydney, Turku, Vienna, Vilnius and Warsaw.

Judging from the people I've met on my travels, it's obvious that instead of globalization we should talk of 'creole-ization'. The people I photograph live on different continents, speak different languages and most of them have never met each other, but – thanks in large part to the internet – they all share the lust for customizing their identities with fragments of culture from different parts of the world. I call this phenomenon 'New Creole Culture'. Its members, far from being clones or victims of globalization, eagerly seek out sites like mine and taste the international cocktail of styles on offer, treating them as inspiration rather than swallowing them whole.

The internet has ended the monopoly on information by the elite – nowadays, even a teenager in a small town in Serbia can be as well informed as Barack Obama or Carine Roitfeld. Online blogs are doing the same thing to fashion. The inspiration process is no longer vertical like it was back in the days when the industry would create the new trends and looks for the masses to imitate. We've reached a point where there's no more top-tier and bottom-rung, no more 'high fashion vs. high street'. Instead of following trends, people prefer to set their own. They've come to expect more from fashion than a list of orders to be obeyed.

This love for the custom-made, intensely individual look has grown noticeably since 2001, when the invention of the iPod began allowing people to update playlists constantly and to juxtapose the complete contents of their music collections. 'What kind of music are you listening to? – A bit of everything!' The iPod generation takes this same chameleon-like approach to fashion, exploring the many facets of their personalities with radically different looks, or customizing their individual styles with elements from different eras and cultures.

So it's superficial to think that young people around the world are all starting to look the same. I believe that we live in a historic time of personal inventiveness, and that human beings have never before been so intensely individual and so interested in dressing creatively. Everyone is becoming their own micro-state, their own style curator and finally, truly, themselves. Trends are dead, baby! Nietzsche's exhortation, 'Become what you are,' is now a reality.

Yvan Rodic,
FACE HUNTER

▸ SINGAPORE Ann Siang Hill November ▾ SYDNEY Surry Hills October

▼ **REYKJAVIK** Downtown August ▶ **LONDON** Brick Lane June

Previous spread
LEFT **REYKJAVIK** Downtown July
RIGHT **REYKJAVIK** Grettisgata July

◄ **STOCKHOLM** Götgatan July ▲ **MEXICO CITY** Fashion Week April

Many street photographers are magnetically drawn to brands and keep asking their victims, 'What are you wearing?' Who cares! I'm not writing a shopping guide.

▼ **MEXICO CITY** Fashion Week April   ◄   ▶ **MELBOURNE** Prahran November

▼ **LONDON** *Soho* December ◄ **HELSINKI Kamppi** July

▼ **BERLIN Mitte** December ▶ **NEW YORK Fashion Week** September

▼ **NEW YORK** Fashion Week September ◀ **SYDNEY** Surry Hills Market November

◄ **LONDON** Soho April ▼ **EMMABODA** Emmaboda Festival August

▲ **REYKJAVIK** Daisy Season July ▶ **NEW YORK** Fashion Week September

◄ **STOCKHOLM** Slussen May ▲ **LONDON** Soho August

► **NEW YORK** Fashion Week September
▼ **MELBOURNE** Vintage fair at the Carlton Club November

I'm not a social scientist or a journalist. This young man is not representative of any particular kind of Berlin style. He's a special case. My pictures are not meant to document reality; they are meant to tell you short stories.

▲ **SYDNEY** Fringe Bar Market November ▶ **LONDON** Brick Lane January

▼ **LONDON** Shoreditch June ▶ **LONDON** Brick Lane Market February

▲ **LONDON** Brick Lane Market April ▶ **BERLIN** Mauerpark July

▲ **LONDON** Fashion Week October ▶ **PARIS** Fashion Week September

◄ **LONDON** Brick Lane June   ▲ **LONDON** Shoreditch December

It's not a cliché – in London you find more cool cats than anywhere else.

▲ **PARIS** Men's Fashion Week January ▶ **MADRID** Malasaña June

◄ **COPENHAGEN** Fashion Week August ▲ **LONDON** Soho September

I want everything but a circus.
People wearing clowny costumes like they do in *FRUiTS* are not my cup of tea.

◀ **COPENHAGEN** Peblinge Sø July ▲ **LONDON** Soho June

Following spread, clockwise from top left
LONDON Gareth Pugh's Halloween party November
LONDON Fashion Week February
STOCKHOLM Fashion Week by Berns July
COPENHAGEN Fashion Week August
MELBOURNE Flinders Street Station November 63

◄ **NEW YORK** Fashion Week September ▲ **LONDON** Shoreditch March

▲ **LONDON** Ramillies Place December ▶ **LONDON** Soho August

▲ **LONDON** Brick Lane Market May ▶ **PARIS** Fashion Week September

Today in Branson Canyon the singer from Io Echo is showing me her favourite place to write songs: the Batcave where the *Batman* television series was shot in the 1960s. I haven't met anyone superficial in LA yet. I'd love to, at least one.

Please, someone come to me!

◄ **MOSCOW** Krysha Mira April ▲ **PARIS** Men's Fashion Week July

▲ PARIS Fashion Week February ▶ PARIS Fashion Week February

▲ **LONDON** Fashion Week February ▶ **LONDON** Soho May

◄ **SÃO PAULO** Fashion Week January ▲ **BERLIN** Fashion Week July

▲ **LONDON** Brick Lane June ▶ **MADRID** Malasaña May

▲ **BERLIN** Bread & Butter show, Tempelhof Airport July ▶ **SÃO PAULO** Fashion Week January

▲ **EMMABODA** Emmaboda Festival August ▶ **MEXICO CITY** Centro Histórico April

When a girl is with her boyfriend, it can sometimes be tricky to ask her for a picture. I usually talk to both of them so no one feels excluded. There's often some kind of 'I'm-sure-he-wants-to-steal-my-girlfriend' tension in the air, but it's usually fine. The worst scenario is when the boyfriend is following me and the girl like a security guard during the shoot, telling his girlfriend how to pose and me how to photograph.

▲ **LONDON** Shoreditch September ▶ **PARIS** Saint-Germain-des-Prés December

▲ **STOCKHOLM** F12 Terassens Invigningsfest May ▶ **OSLO** Aker Brygge December

▲ **LONDON** Fashion Week February ▶ **LONDON** Tottenham Court Road May

◄ **SYDNEY** Oxford Street November ▲ **WARSAW** Śródmieście October

▲ **LONDON** Brick Lane June ▶ **NEW YORK** SoHo August

▲ **LONDON** Fashion Week February ▶ **LONDON** Soho April

I get my best shots when there's time for my models to play around and have fun.

▲ **LONDON** Fashion Week February ▶ **LONDON** Brick Lane March

▲ **LONDON** Brick Lane April ▶ **LONDON** Fitzrovia March

▲ **LONDON** Tottenham Court Road January ▶ **NEW YORK** SoHo August

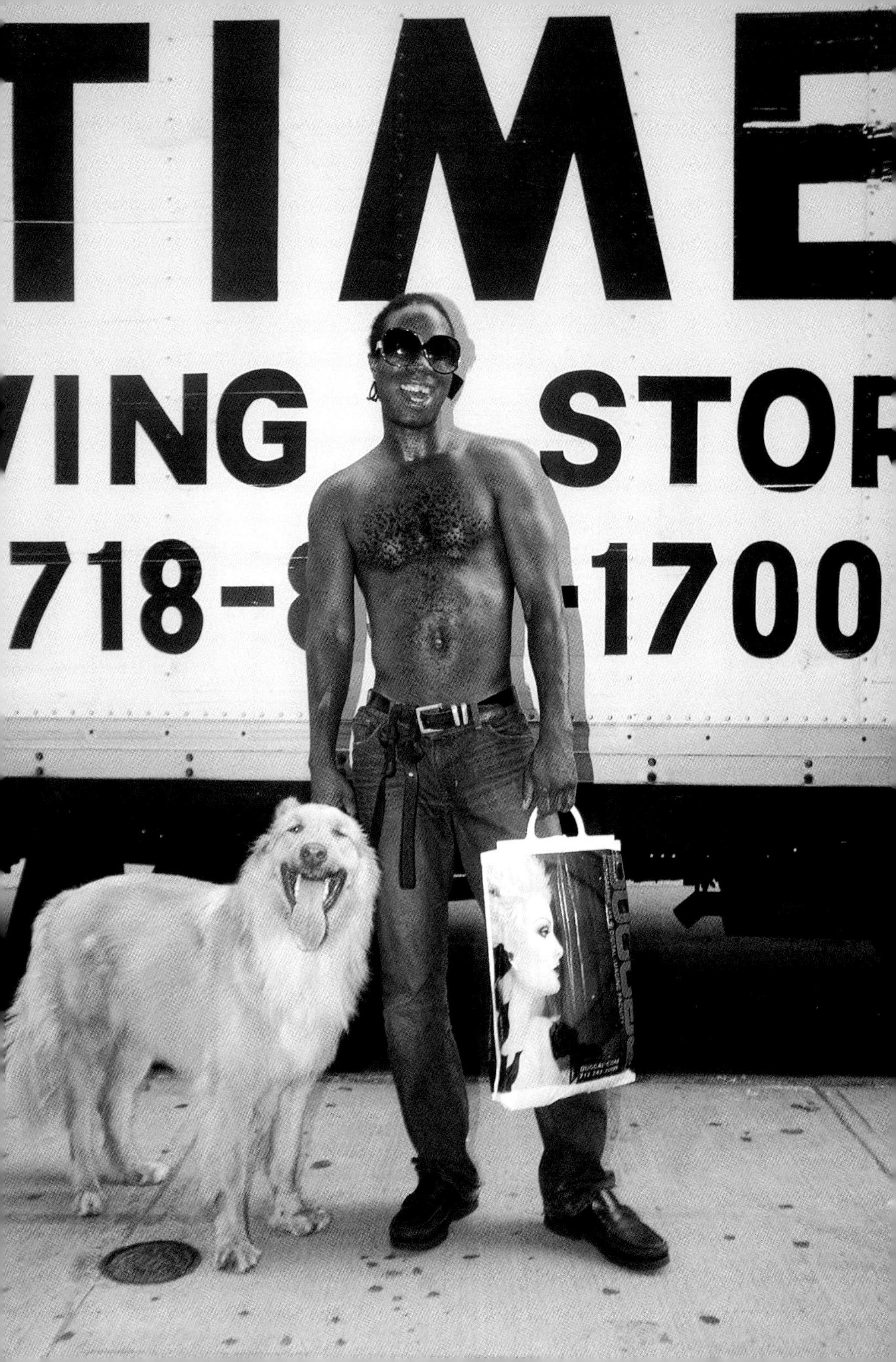
TIME
VING STOR
718-8 -1700

▲ **LONDON** Shoreditch May ▶ **REYKJAVIK** Iceland Airwaves Festival October

◄ **LONDON** Brick Lane December ▲ **PARIS** Men's Fashion Week January

◄ **LONDON** Brick Lane December ▲ **STOCKHOLM** Fashion Week by Berns July

▲ **SÃO PAULO** Mario Queiroz Party at the Sofitel January
▶ **COPENHAGEN** On the Street August

This is one of my best memories. I met the Danish-Brazilian artist Yaya at a surreal hotel party in São Paulo. In the main suite they had this pool full of plastic balls, but everyone was too shy to play in it. Yaya and I and another girl were the only ones who jumped straight in.

Looking a little confused, the party crowd stared at us as we played like kids.

▲ **PARIS** Men's Fashion Week June ▶ **PARIS** Le Marais April

I know designers at Dior who check my blog because they don't have time to go out on the street. I'm not knowledgable about fashion – I can't identify a Chanel dress from 1967 – so it's funny that I can have a tiny influence on such a big business.

▲ **LONDON** Soho May ▶ **LONDON** Brick Lane April

◄ NEW YORK Fashion Week September ▲ LONDON Soho June

▲ **LOS ANGELES** Downtown April ▶ **PARIS** Terrace of Au Printemps August

▲ **PARIS** Fashion Week October ▶ **REYKJAVIK** Nordic Fashion Biennale March

Following spread
LEFT **NEW YORK** Fashion Week September
RIGHT **PARIS** Fashion Week March

◄ **LONDON** Soho September ▲ **KIEV** Ukrainian Fashion Week March

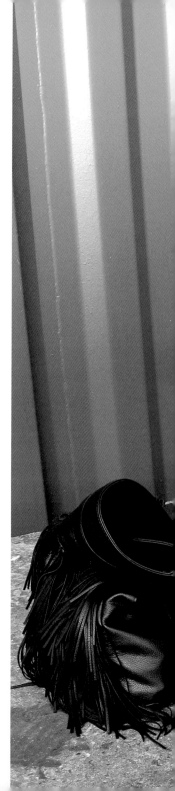

◀ **REYKJAVIK** Menningarnótt August ▲ **PARIS** Fashion Week March

Previous spread, clockwise from top left
LONDON Soho June **LONDON** Marylebone May **SÃO PAULO** Fashion Week June
LONDON Brick Lane January **ANTWERP** Royal Academy of Fine Arts April
COACHELLA Coachella Festival April **LONDON** Shoreditch September

▲ **LONDON** Soho June ▶ **LONDON** Soho March

▲ PARIS Men's Fashion Week June ▶ REYKJAVIK Downtown July

▲ **PARIS** Men's Fashion Week June ▶ **LONDON** Fitzrovia May

LOS ANGELES Mid-City April

Tango mid-city with CC in the sunshine. That night it was Medusa Lounge and La Boom at Bardot; in the morning, a fresh-fruit breakfast in the middle of the desert on the way to Coachella.

From now on LA is going to be on my list of the top five most liveable cities in the world.

Following spread
LEFT **REYKJAVIK** Iceland Airwaves Festival October
RIGHT **PARIS** Men's Fashion Week January

◄ **LONDON** Soho May ▲ **NEW YORK** Fashion Week September

The only secret is to wear what you feel and what fits you.
Fashion is what you buy, style is what you are. 167

▲ **LONDON** Brick Lane June ▶ **ANTWERP** Royal Academy of Fine Arts April

◂ PARIS Fashion Week September ▴ COACHELLA Coachella Festival April

▲ **LONDON** Chalk Farm August ▶ **BARCELONA** Raval August

I never understood why fashion editors waste so much time and money flying bland professional models halfway around the world for a photoshoot. Their lives would be much less complicated if they worked like me: travel to a great city, find a stylish natural beauty who lives around the corner, bring her to the playground and play on the slides, give the children candy to get them out of the way, hit the shoot button. Five minutes later you're done and can go relax on the *terrasse*.

◄ **PARIS** Fashion Week March ▲ **PARIS** Franklin D. Roosevelt Métro station January

Previous spread

LEFT **HAMBURG** Alster February RIGHT **COPENHAGEN** Islands Brygge December

▲ **HELSINKI** Antti Asplund sale July ▶ **LONDON** Brick Lane February

◄ **LONDON** Cavendish Square May   ▲ **COPENHAGEN** In the Parks July

▲ **PARIS** Fashion Week September ▶ **REYKJAVIK** Iceland Airwaves Festival October

◄ **WARSAW** Marszalkowska March ▲ **BUCHAREST** Vitan October

▲ **STOCKHOLM** Slussen January ▶ **ÅRHUS** Harbour May

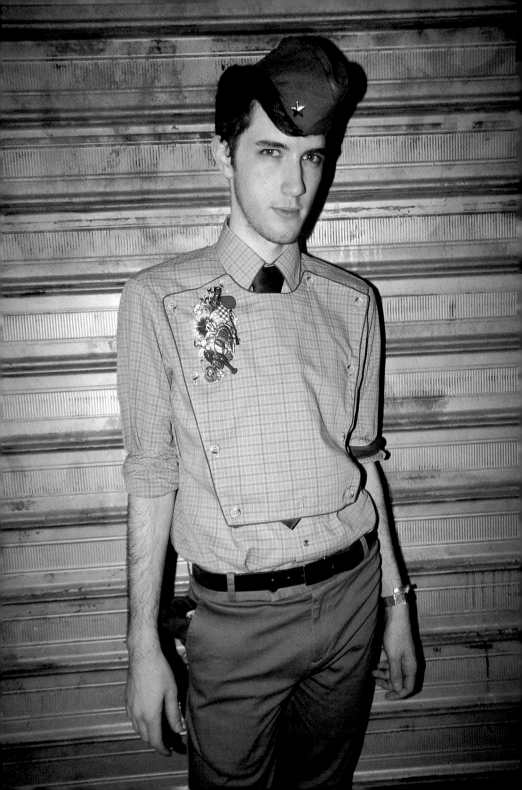

▲ LONDON Fashion Week February
◄ NEW YORK Michael Ricardo Andreev opening at BBlessing, Lower East Side February

◄ **LONDON** Brick Lane Market December ▲ **LONDON** Spitalfields May

Following spread, clockwise from top left
PARIS Fashion Week March **JAKARTA** Selamat Tinggal December **LONDON** West End March
PARIS Fashion Week October **HELSINKI** Bum Bum at Rose Garden June
BERLIN New Year's Eve December **STOCKHOLM** Södermalm May **LONDON** Soho May

▼ **PARIS** Men's Fashion Week June   ▶ **PARIS** Fashion Week October

▲ **PARIS** Place Vendôme October ▶ **STOCKHOLM** Södermalm October

I photograph the people who seduce me. You can't seduce me with an It-bag or a pair of It-shoes. Sorry, guys – I don't know much about fashion. I'm more interested in personality, charisma, madness and creativity.

◄ **LONDON** Shoreditch May ▲ **COPENHAGEN** Nørreport July

I want people to do a double-take and say:
'What's going on? This girl looks so amazing – and she's standing in front of that!'

I want them to wonder whether it's real or a setup. Street style is supposed to be
spontaneous, but sometimes I try to organize a picture so that it's just on the edge of
looking real.

◄ **WARSAW** Marszalkowska March ▲ **LONDON** Fashion Week September

▲ **BERLIN** Prenzlauer Berg December ▶ **NEW YORK** Fashion Week September

◄ **LOS ANGELES** Hollywood April ▲ **LONDON** West End April

I met Rachel the night before at the Standard Hotel. I'd just had a call
from a band cancelling their interview for my web-TV programme.
I saw her next to the pool and asked for a picture.

She told me she was playing in a band; I asked her if she was free the next day,
and she was. We met at her family's house in Hollywood where she played
with her folk band, He's My Brother, She's My Sister. Magic.

▲ **LONDON** Brick Lane November ▸ **PARIS** Fashion Week September

◄ **COACHELLA** Coachella Festival April ▲ **LONDON** Brick Lane September

Previous spread, clockwise from top left
COACHELLA Coachella Festival April **LONDON** White City May
MELBOURNE Cup Day, Flemington November **COPENHAGEN** Fashion Week August

◄ **LONDON** Brick Lane February ▲ **LONDON** Brick Lane February

▲ **TURKU** Uuden Musiikin Festivaali July ▶ **BERLIN** Fashion Week July

◄ **PARIS** Fashion Week February ▲ **HELSINKI** On the Street January

▲ PARIS Men's Fashion Week June ▶ PARIS Men's Fashion Week June

▲ **SYDNEY** Paddington November ▶ **SYDNEY** Paddington November

◄ **PARIS** Fashion Week February ▲ **NEW YORK** Fashion Week September

◄ PARIS Fashion Week October   ▲ LONDON Brick Lane August

239

▲ **PARIS** Fashion Week February ▶ **SYDNEY** Bondi Beach November

▲ **BUCHAREST** My Grandma's Backyard at the Museum of the Romanian Peasant October
◄ **STOCKHOLM** Fashion Week by Berns January

▲ STOCKHOLM F12 Terrasens Invigningsfest May
▶ LONDON Great Marlborough Street November

You can try to reduce it down to a formula, but I don't know why certain people catch my eye. Someone could spend ten hours on the blog and decide 'Oh, he likes this kind of hair, and if I wear this kind of shoes he'll take my picture.' Maybe I will – but maybe not. There are no rules. I love to surprise myself.

▲ **LONDON** Soho February ▶ **GOTHENBURG** Haga Nygata August

◄ **NEW YORK** SoHo August   ▲ **LONDON** Soho March

▲ **STOCKHOLM** Fashion Week by Berns June ▶ **LONDON** Brick Lane March

▲ **LONDON** Soho April ▸ **STOCKHOLM** Götgatsbacken May

The first picture that was on my blog I took randomly, not knowing I would have a blog. Now I'm more selective. I can spend five hours in a city and not get a single shot if I don't see anything that really 'shocks' me. When I finally spot the right person, I try to build my picture in a composition. It usually means walking around to find the appropriate background. So it's more like an improvised photo-shoot.

▲ **PARIS** Fashion Week October ▶ **LONDON** Brick Lane December

▲ **REYKJAVIK** Menningarnótt August
◄ **EMMABODA** Emmaboda Festival August

For the huge majority of human beings,
it's easier to relate to beautiful normal people
than to skinny tall models wearing $30,000 outfits.

◄ ÅRHUS Toldkammeret May   ▼ BUDAPEST Lánchíd May

◄ **STOCKHOLM** Södermalm May ▲ **SYDNEY** Paddington October

I find it equally interesting to take the portraits of kids in a music festival in Iceland, artists in a gallery show in Miami Beach, cyclists on the street in Melbourne or stylists at Paris Fashion Week.

▲ **PARIS** Fashion Week March ▶ **REYKJAVIK** Suðurlandsvegur July

◄ **NEW YORK** Fashion Week September   ▲ **NEW YORK** Fashion Week September

◄ **LONDON** Marylebone April ▲ **EDINBURGH** The Meadows May

▲ **STOCKHOLM** Medborgarplatsen May
▶ **HELSINKI** Kamppi July

The city is no longer just an asphalt jungle –
it's become a close friend we like to hang out with.

◄ **LOS ANGELES** Fairfax Flea Market April ▲ **STOCKHOLM** Fashion Week by Berns June

277

So many commercials show people expressing fake emotions that in
the 21st century it's difficult to trust authentic gestures in photographs.
But trust me – I didn't ask these two people to 'show me love'.

Following spread
LEFT **LONDON** Soho April   RIGHT **BERLIN** Dircksenstrasse May

▲ **LONDON** Shoreditch November   ▶ **LONDON** Brick Lane March

LONDON Brick Lane March

British street style is without a doubt the most influential in the world. London is like a mysterious laboratory where new cultural movements are perpetually invented.

You find people copying Londoners in every country, but you will never see a Londoner following the aesthetic of another capital city.

▲ **PARIS** Men's Fashion Week January ▶ **MUNICH** Spielbar Tragbar June

Previous spread, clockwise from top left
LONDON Brick Lane January
MELBOURNE CBD November   **LONDON** Fashion Week February
LONDON Brick Lane April   **LONDON** Brick Lane August

◄ **COPENHAGEN** Nørrebro June ▲ **REYKJAVIK** Iceland Airwaves Festival October

▲ **PARIS** Pont des Arts January ▶ **GOTHENBURG** On the Street October

▲ **LONDON** Brick Lane April ▶ **LONDON** Soho February

▲ **REYKJAVIK** Nordic Fashion Biennale March ▶ **LONDON** Brick Lane January

◄ **LONDON** Tottenham Court Road September ▲ **MELBOURNE** CBD November

▲ **LONDON** Fitzrovia October ▸ **LONDON** Shoreditch July

Following spread
LEFT **WARSAW** Śródmieście October RIGHT **LONDON** On the Street April

▲ COPENHAGEN Fashion Week August ▶ BERLIN Prenzlauer Berg December

◄ **STOCKHOLM** Fashion Week by Berns January ▲ **LONDON** Soho April

▲ **PARIS** Fashion Week March ▶ **SYDNEY** Darlinghurst October

◄ **LONDON** Argyll Street January ▲ **MEXICO CITY** Fashion Week April

▲ **REYKJAVIK** Iceland Airwaves Festival October
▶ **SINGAPORE** Ann Siang Hill Park November

My blog is like a diary of my moods.
My friends sometimes check my pictures
to see if I'm down or having a good time.

Now stop staring at me, and close the book!

Yvan Rodic, the photographer behind Facehunter.com, one of

ANTWERP BARCELONA BERLIN

the fashion world's most visited street style blogs, has compiled

BUCHAREST BUDAPEST COPENHAGEN

in this book images that show his unerring sensibility for street style.

GLASGOW HELSINKI ISTANBUL JAKARTA

He has captured real people, whose clothes reflect their character,

LONDON KIEV LOS ANGELES MADRID

charisma and confidence. The result is a portfolio of what's chic on the

MELBOURNE MEXICO CITY MOSCOW

street and an insightful predictor of what will be chic on the runway.

MUNICH NEW YORK OSLO PARIS

Whether you're fashion forward, backward, or sideways, you'll find

REYKJAVIK SÃO PAULO SINGAPORE

something inspiring in this radical, personal and unpredictable book.

STOCKHOLM SYDNEY WARSAW